# INVENTORY

## POETRY BY DIONNE BRAND

*'Fore Day Morning* (1978)

*Earth Magic* (for children 1980/1993/2006)

*Winter Epigrams and Epigrams to
Ernesto Cardenal in Defense of Claudia* (1983)

*Primitive Offensive* (1983)

*Chronicles of the Hostile Sun* (1984)

*No Language Is Neutral* (1990)

*Land to Light On* (1997)

*thirsty* (2002)

*Inventory* (2006)

# INVENTORY

## Dionne Brand

McCLELLAND & STEWART

**Library and Archives Canada Cataloguing in Publication**

Brand, Dionne
Inventory / Dionne Brand.

Poems.

ISBN 13: 978-0-7710-1662-2
ISBN 10: 0-7710-1662-X

I. Title.

PS8553.R275I58 2006    C811'.54    C2005-906043-3

We acknowledge the financial support of the Government of Canada through the Book Publishing Industry Development Program and that of the Government of Ontario through the Ontario Media Development Corporation's Ontario Book Initiative. We further acknowledge the support of the Canada Council for the Arts and the Ontario Arts Council for our publishing program.

Typeset in Bembo by M&S, Toronto
Printed and bound in Canada

This book is printed on acid-free paper that is 100% recycled, ancient-forest friendly (100% post-consumer recycled).

McClelland & Stewart Ltd.
75 Sherbourne Street
Toronto, Ontario
M5A 2P9
www.mcclelland.com

1  2  3  4  5      10  09  08  07  06

# INVENTORY

I

We believed in nothing

the black-and-white american movies
buried themselves in our chests,
glacial, liquid, acidic as love

the way to Wyoming, the sunset in Cheyenne,
the surreptitious cook fires, the uneasy
sleep of cowboys, the cactus, the tumbleweed,
the blankets,
the homicides of Indians,
lit, dimmed, lit, dimmed

lit in the drawing rooms,
the suicides inside us

and the light turnings to stone,
inside and out,
we arrived spectacular, tendering
our own bodies into dreamery,
as meat, as mask, as burden

like chaos

all the fake feelings we had, oh love,
the acts of ventriloquism, the wooded arteries,
the arms clattering to the floor,
the big raw cities flailing us

we returned home dead on our feet
and melancholy

the earth was never the earth,
we were never anyone,
everything we were preceded us,
foolish in the heady days
when we thought we might, somehow
within a few seasons,
after their laughter and raucid whistles

but this was their manifesto,
and we took it like fun,
the burnt kernels, the chemical sugars

their love stories never contained us,
their war epics left us bloody

we poor, we weak, we dying

we cheered them,
encouraged them, helped them with the cooking,
the tracking to our throat lines,
gave them the books of signs,
the last magical bird feather,
the traces of our fires

the screens lacerate our intimacies
gathered at the windows

on the corners, thinking one day
we'll make it, delicately,
without a war, without the tragedy
of it all
and maybe with our bodies,
though now

it's too late for that

We waited, we waited sticklike and nervous,
did what we could when allowed

made up all the dances, fine,
burned our lungs on music,
so many dead musicians,
the extraterrestrial neurons, the brittle veins it took
to leave so much music, so much music,
so much dried muscle at olympian lines,
the heels eviscerated with speed

and all the folded linen, all
the broken fingers, pricked and bruised,
misformed ribs and the famished babies
for the world's most famous photos

the steel we poured, the rivets we fastened
to our bare bones like cars,
we stripped, so fastidious,
the seams of dirt excised from apples and gold

all the railways

everywhere, and the forests we destroyed,
as far as
the Amazonas' forehead, the Congo's gut,
the trees we peeled of rough butter,
full knowing, there's something wrong
with this

then the prison couture of orange-clad criminals
we became,
the kinkiness of blindfolds we admitted

we did all this and more

there were roads of viscera and supine alphabets,
and well, fields of prostration,
buildings mechanized with flesh and acreages
of tender automobiles

heavy with our tiredness, solid with our devotion

after work we succumbed
headlong in effusive rooms

to the science-fiction tales of democracy
and to their songs,
*come gather 'round people     for the times*
*say it loud     and when you talk about destruction*
*count me out     deep in my heart I do believe*
*oh lord won't you buy me     make me wanna holler*

that's fine, got drunk, got high,
said we were already living in another time

they waited, watched,
evacuated all our good lyrics
of the goodness, of the science, the delicious
being of more than, well more,
so hard now to separate what was them

from what we were

how imprisoned we are in their ghosts

how in their beginnings and endings
no wonder, no wonder,
every evening falls on axioms,
the violins of edible fears

someone enters in black, oh darling, oh love,
the eclipses of windowpanes,
the secret life of the sun's corona going by

the woman is lying in the alleyway

treacherous and naked once more,

half the mind is atrophied in this,
just as inanimate doors and pickup trucks,
the unremitting malls of all desires

small years, small for the distancing planet,
how would we know, so suspended, defenceless
with our hungers,
nibbling our own hearts to the red pits

how would it truly be to have danced
with Celia Cruz, unsmiling

to have studied instead
the street names of Montevideo or Havana,
Kingston and Caracas as if planning to live there
in the elegant future, as if no other life would do,
or if the vows of transformation
were only made in Parral or Basse-Pointe

to have loved instead
*Te recuerdo Amanda, la calle mojada,*
*corriendo a la fábrica    la lluvia en el pelo,*
to sing this to potential lovers

then to have seen Che
Guevara as an old man on television,

Angela's unbreakable voice has made jails extinct,
to die in this compassion,
to have never heard "Redemption Song," so hoarse, at all

not willing another empire but history's pulse
measured with another hand,
as continents roll over in their sleep

a whimsical contraption moved with sometimish winds

of inconvenient magnets to allow
unpredictable openings of incurable light

now we must wait on their exhaustion, now
we have to pray for their demise with spiked hands,
with all the brilliant silences,
to understand the whole language,
the whole immaculate language of the ravaged world

II

Observed over Miami, the city, an orange slick blister,
the houses, stiff-haired organisms clamped to the earth,
engorged with oil and wheat,
rubber and metals,
the total contents of the brain, the electrical
regions of the atmosphere, water

coming north, reeling, a neurosis of hinged
clouds,
bodies thicken, flesh

out in immodest health,
six boys, fast food on their breath,
luscious paper bags, the perfume of grilled offal,
troughlike cartons of cola,
a gorgon luxury of electronics, backward caps,
bulbous clothing, easy hearts '

lines of visitors are fingerprinted,
eye-scanned, grow murderous,
then there's the business of thoughts
who can glean with any certainty,
the guards, blued and leathered, multiply
to stop them,
palimpsests of old borders, the sea's graph on the skin,
the dead giveaway of tongues,
soon, soon, the implants to discern lies

from the way a body moves

there's that already

she felt ill, wanted
to murder the six boys, the guards,
the dreamless shipwrecked
burning their beautiful eyes in the patient queue

Let's go to the republic of home,
let's forget all this then, this victorious procession,
these blenching queues,
this timeless march of nails in shoeless feet

what people will take and give,
the passive lines, the passive guards,
if passivity can be inchoate self-loathing

all around, and creeping

self-righteous, let's say it, fascism,
how else to say, border,
and the militant consumption of everything,
the encampment of the airport, the eagerness
to be all the same, to mince biographies
to some exact phrases, some
exact and toxic genealogy

III

One year she sat at the television weeping,
no reason,
the whole time

and the next, and the next

the wars' last and late night witness,
some she concluded are striving on grief
and burnt clothing, bloody rags, bomb-filled shoes

the pitiful domestic blankets
in the hospitals,
the bundles of plump
corpses waiting or embraced by screams,
the leaking chests and ridiculous legs

the abrupt density of life gone out, the
manifold substances of stillness

nothing personal is recorded here,
you must know that, but
one year the viciousness got to be too much

the news was advertisement for movies,
the movies were the real killings

the baked precipitous ditches,
twisted metal hulks of things that used to be,
fires intense as black holes, voids in schoolyards
and hotels, in kitchens and prophetic boys

all this became ordinary far from where it happened

the Arab faces were Arab faces after all,
not even the western hostages were hostages,
the lives of movie stars were more lamentable,
and the wreckage of streets was unimportant

what confidences would she tell you then,
what would possibly be safe in your hands

but never mind that, here is the latest watchful hour

– twenty-seven in Hillah, three in fighting in
Amariya, two by roadside bombing, Adhaim,
five by mortars in Afar, in firefight in Samarra

two, two in collision near Khallis, council member
in Kirkuk, one near medical complex, two in
Talafar, five by suicide bomb in Kirkuk, five

by suicide in Shorgat, one in attack on police
chief, Buhurz, five by car bomb in Baquba,
policeman in Mosul, two by car bomb, Madaen

five by mortars in Talafar, Sufi follower
near Baghdad, twelve by suicide bomb in
restaurant, bystander in Dora, in Mishada,
in Hillah, twenty-seven again, twenty-seven –

she's heard clearly now, twenty-three,
by restaurant bomb near green zone, Ibn Zanbour,
and so clear, syntonic, one, threading a needle

three beating dust from slippers, anyone looking
for a newspaper, an idea in their head like figs will soon
be in season, four playing dominoes, drinking Turkish coffee

seven by shop window, with small girl, in wading pool,
twelve half naked by river, nine shot dead in

Missouri shopping mall, possible yes, in restaurant
in Madison, three nephews, one aunt in Nashville fire bomb,
six by attack near hospital in Buffalo, two listening to radio

sixteen by bomb at football stadium, one reading
on bus "the heart is enclosed in a pericardial sac
that is lined with the parietal layers of serous membrane . . ."

three with the electricity gone since Thursday,
still fumbling for candles then finding the matches

beating on the tympanic bone, by suicide bomb,
by suicide bomb, by car bomb, by ambush, any
number by sunlight, in daylight, by evening

still on those safe streets, amber alerts go out
by television, by puppetry, in sessions of paranoia,
in heavy suits with papers in cool hands as if staring at fools

there are announcements of imagined disturbances,
of dreads and sometimes it must be play, surely,
and the peculiar fragility of power

where it's the safest they use yellow and amber
and red pretending like the movies that there's
a bad guy every sixty seconds, and a car chase
coming and a hero with fire power

still in June,
in their hiatus eight killed by suicide bomb at
bus station, at least eleven killed in Shula at
restaurants, at least fifteen by car bomb, Irbil

At least someone should stay awake, she thinks,
someone should dream them along the abysmal roads

twenty-three by suicide bomb at Ibn Zanbour kebab
restaurant, no need to repeat this really, just the name
of the kebab place is new, isn't it

enough numbers still to come so twenty
outside bank in Kirkuk, the numbers so random,
so shapeless, apart from their shape, their seduction of infinity

the ganglia and meninges, the grey matter
of the cerebrum, the viscous peritoneal cavity

did she say two listening to the radio, to Nancy Amriq perhaps
any, any, preferring by sleep, by magic, in hallucinations

but here it is in rush hour, in traffic, a queue near the scarf
seller, in a moment's inattention, injured by petals of nails,
and hot wire, fugitive valves, a rain of small glittering teeth

and bones beatific, sharpened with heat, at least

it was sudden if not predictable at any rate
not on Sunset Boulevard, Potsdame Strasse,
Oxford Circus, Rue du Faubourg St. Honore and
all those streets

of reasonable suspicion, of self-fulfilling
dread, charred by home improvements,
self-makeovers, what goes for conscience now

what foundations, what animus calms, we're
doing the best we can with these people,
what undeniable hatred fuels them, what else
can we do, nothing but maim them,

we do not deserve it, it's out of the blue,
the sleeplessness at borders, the poor sunlight,
the paralyzed cars, they hate our freedom,

they want the abominable food from our mouths

"It is worst during the night
when the bombardment is most intense"

look, where are the matches, no, don't light a fire,
the tap's dripping precious,
the electricity will soon come back, how far
away is it now, the phosphorescent bodies,
the tremulous wounded hallways

she has to keep watch at the window
of the television, she hears what is never shown,
the details are triumphant,
she'll never be able the write them in time

the paper now, and where's the hair oil,
the butter's gone rancid,
remember that cat we used to have,
it disappeared the first day,
lemons, remember to buy lemons

there's another life, she listens, each hour, each night,
behind the flat screen and the news anchor,
the sleek, speeding cars, the burgers, the breaking

celebrity news, unrealities of faraway islands,
bickering and spiteful,
each minute so drastic, they win a million dollars

the waiting, she can't bear the waiting,
the metal, metal, metal of waiting,
she sits devoted, the pairing knife close
to a harvest of veins

now everything is in her like ends and tastes,
the loosening clasp of affinities
everyone grows perversely accustomed,
she refuses

If they're numb over there, and all around her,
she'll gather the nerve endings
spilled on the streets, she'll count them like rice grains

she'll keep them for when they're needed

for music and the ornaments of air without bombing,
for bread and honey, the kilos of figs
in December and baked yams from burnt

fingered vendors, the washing to be done,
the sewing, the bicycles to be repaired,
the daily lists to be made of mundane
matters, like the cost of sugar, or the girl losing
her new pencils again

and not to say, for the memories of the forgetful, the
spinners of silences,
the teethed impasto of broadcasts

she'll gather the passions of women,
their iron feet, their bitter hair, their
perpetual nuptial assignment

to battered kitchens and rooms
radiant with their blood vessels

their waiting at doors
at night in the universe, such waiting

the mind surpasses, the bones are a failure,
the pregnancies wretched again, and again

she'll store the nerves' endings in glass
coloured bottles on a tree near the doorsteps,
for divine fierce years to come

when the planet is ruined, the continent
forlorn in water and smoke

till then
where are the packages of black pepper,
the oil for the lilac bore, the shovel

if she wakes up tomorrow and things are still this way,
then the shovel for the ice
in the garden, the winter-eaten sidewalk

someone died leaving her a basket,
she'll fill it with the overflow,
line it with day lilies and the wine
she makes sitting there
pressing and pressing these bundles of dried blooms

the bus stations are empty and sobbing,
the unemployment lines are runny
like broken eggs, the construction sites
pile up endlessly, nothing is finished

she is a woman who is losing the idea
of mathematics,
the maximum is so small, the
crushed spines of vehicles fly in the air,
all September, all October

where's the flour, the nighttime stories, where's
the sugar for the tongue's amusement, muscle
and likeness,

now she wishes she could hear
all that noise that poets make about
time and timelessness

come throw some water on her forehead,
look for the butterflies so wingless,
the oven is freezing with a steady, steady cold

Stay now, she's written a letter,
an account of her silence,
its destination all the streets
beginning with Al Kifah, Al Rashid,
Abu Nuwas, Hafa, Mansur, and the 14th of July

beginning – what door are you looking through now,
still what door are you looking through,
what sound does the world make there,
the sound you must have heard
before these disasters, the sound
you must keep

don't pray it only makes things worse, I know,
think instead of what we might do
and why, why are only the men in the streets,
all over the world

the houses are on the edge of rotted dreams,
all the dictators' palaces are made of the same wood

if I say in this letter, I'm waiting
to step into another life,
will you come then and find me

without rivers, without hopes, without nails,
without anything we now know, without
bruises, without bullet-holed walls

will you come without news of confessions
of serial killers and lost brides?

let us forget all that, let us not act surprised,
or make coy distinctions among mass
murderers, why ration nuclear weapons,
let us all celebrate death

when you come though we'll listen
to Coltrane's *Stellar Regions*, to water,
to rain, again, anywhere, and to Betty Carter

to caterpillars gnawing at leaves,
to gira cooking in oil, to all the songs
I love and have forgotten like Smokey
Robinson's "Ooh Baby Baby" and Roaring Lion's
"Caroline," we'll just listen

the ear is so valuable, it is like sleep

to Dinah Washington and Leonard Cohen,
to Fairuz, to yawning and to one bee eating fruit

what time do you like best, whenever,
the best thing then is the Atlantic, wherever
you find it, then you don't need music,
it is the beginning of music

Cecil Taylor knows this, and Kathleen Battle
and Fateh Ali Khan, and Abdullah Ibrahim,
then just watching that ocean evens out the world

all I can offer you now though is my brooding hand,
my sodden eyelashes and the like,
these humble and particular things I know,
my eyes pinned to your face

understand, I will keep you alive like this,
the desolate air between us is no match
for the brittle orchids we are destined to eat together,
the ashen tulips we will devour voraciously

take this letter, put it on your tongue,
sleep while I keep watch,
know that I am your spy here, your terrorist,
find me

Days, moored to the freight of this life,
the ordnances of her brooding hands, the
abacus of her eyelids

thirteen drowned off the coast of Italy,
nine by car bomb in Amarah, twenty by
suicide in Baghdad, child on bicycle by bomb
in Baquba

why does that alliterate on its own, why
does she observe the budding of that consonant

demonstrator shot dead in Samarra,
woman in mortar attack in Mosul,
five poultry dealers shot dead in Yusufiyah

two men and child by car bomb,
TV news director in Sayyidiyya, twenty-one
cockle pickers by drowning at Morecambe Bay

by malaria, by hemorrhagic fevers, by hungers,
by fingerprint, by dogs and vigilantes

by arrests near the tunnel,
in arrest by La Migra in Brewster County,
Hidalgo County, Dona Ana County, and Zapata County

by asylum
in Traiskirchen, at Brussels, at Helsinki,
in deportations to Buenos Aires, Ricardo Barrientos

in childhood at Pagani, at Lampedusa and Regina
Pacis, at Safi army barracks, in three hundred
and ninety-five terrible villages in Darfur – Sisi,
Mangarsal, Artala, Mukjar, Jabel Moon

in documentaries, in liquid surfaces,
in oceanic blue screens, in disappearances in
the secret seas of living rooms here

where's their sweet life of green oranges,
of plums and dates, of papayas ripening

forget it, we can't speak of nature in that breath any more,
the earth is corroding already with cities

then where the cafés with students plotting
rebellion,
wreathed in thin cigarette smoke and flagrant lust,
the brains angry and lovely with doorways

where she lives they go about their business,
carry umbrellas against the drizzled rain of evidence,
the tattoo parlours are full as if making
warriors, but nothing happens

the wealth multiplies in the garbage dumps,
and the quiet is the quiet of thieves

there are cellphones calling no one,
no messages burn on the planet's withered lungs

all that koltan from Kahuzi-Biega, the landslides,
to carry nothing

what about the love notes, what, the absolution of airplanes

it's all empty, she thinks, but then again
that's not news

the mollient burdens carried in knapsacks,
all the footwear and headgear and SUVs,
the anodyne poets of jingles,
the drugstores of painkillers are for this

what next, everything is touched,
the train stations not the least with massive
explosions, and the mind limps to its tribal
impulses

Let us not invoke the natural world,
it's ravaged like any battlefield, like any tourist
island, like any ocean we care to name,
like oxygen

let's at least admit we mean each other
harm,
we intend to do damage

then she may stop this vigil for broken things,
then she can at least sit down
to eat the chrome muscles of grocery carts,
the hearts of ubiquitous concrete barriers

we,
there is no "we"
let us separate ourselves now,
though perhaps we can't, still and again
too late for that,
nothing but to continue

the underground subways are hysterical with gurneys,
and yellow tape and smoked saliva,
the cities wear bandages over the eyes

the conversation is over except,
"we won't change our way of life for this savagery
against civilized nations . . . murders when we talk peace"

whatever language we might have spoken
is so thick with corrupt intentions,
it persuades no one

she's fearful, yes, like anyone,
explosions in Jakarta, the same day,
Ayodhya two days before,
a hurricane moving toward Guantanamo

seems harmless enough
and merely like the hand of God

though ominous rain, the blue seas' limning screens
are saturated with experts on terror

where did they learn this,
where you wonder did such men, ruddy with health,
cultivate this wicked knowledge

then you realize they have an office,
a new industry for the stock exchange
and an expense account, an ardour for subterfuge

they're traders, like anybody else these days,
in what's obvious,
and skilful in half-hourly repetitions
of the same shameless verses

day and night

It was not coincidence then that the day
was beautiful, the highways roaring,
the sky that blue which is deeply ordinary
and infinite

perhaps in this city she was distracted
for a few seconds by the open blinds,
the living room's clarity, the kitchen's decisions,
she'd thought then of going, going somewhere

the six lanes hummed, scratched under the wheel,
the windows of houses going by blinked vacant
through the speed and noise

machine and body, shield and tissue,
the highway worked itself into her shoulders
and neck, now she was trembling, tasting
all the materials the city stuffs in its belly

now she was concrete and car, asphalt and oil,
head whirring like any engine,
becoming what they were all becoming

sunny and hot, sunny and hot, the radio chirped

the same in London, Chicago, Tours, Barcelona,
some rain in St. Elizabeth, Port-au-Prince deluge,
floods in Matanzas, regular day in Melbourne, São Paulo

the physical world is not interested in us,
it does what it does,
its own inventory of time, of light and dark

not faith and doubt, not malice or charm,
inexplicable then our certainty
in the fame of politicians and the blackmail of priests

memory will tell us this was foolish,
only, we're not there

there's laughter on some street in the world, and a baby,
crying same as any street, anywhere, and some say
the world is not the same, but it is you know

now, same as anywhere, still, a baby crying here
may not be about hunger, not that kind of hunger

eating years into the cheeks, making puffed bellows
of the abdomen, ah why invoke that, we know about it

we don't care beyond pity, so the thing is straight and simple,
the suburbs, the outskirts are inevitable

Aulnay-sous-Bois, Jane-Finch, the faithless hyphens,
the electrical yards, the unsociable funereal parking lots
with transparent children and their killing play,
that ravaged world is here

and the day is always beautiful somewhere

does she care "about the human species
spreading out across the cosmos"
no, God forbid, stop them, and forgive her this one
imprecation to a deity

then the expert on the radio said, "It would be
like how they spread across the New World"
the glee and hedonism in his voice

and the man who killed Van Gogh, Mohammed
Bouyeri, said to Van Gogh's mother,
"I have to admit I don't have any sympathy for you,
I can't feel for you because I think you are a non-believer"

That's not a revolution you want, ever, to win,
the theory of nothing, theories of nothing in return

These maples that now sentinel her thoughts
know that, and that river with its irregular susurrus

a highway sighing from its aches at 3 or 4 a.m.
she hears this too,
even Martha's lion with its marble eyes, frozen
of course this north in stone

the evening hummingbird's beak spiralling
through the derangement of a spider's web,
the various last calls of day birds she cannot
name, her left hand, its involuntary tensing,
the city's summer heat at bay in this forest
after hours of driving

the newspapers dishevelled on the floor,
her lover bathing up the stairs,
the cobalt destiny of all skies,
a telephone call to another hemisphere

how is it, how's the coming hurricane,
it's passed, the hurricane just came, yawned
and left

we're here, a bomb went off,
two days ago though, you didn't hear, no,
a dry run they think, a small device, a lady
got hurt

how is it there, only hysteria,
nothing really, okay then, well

the ripples of resignation there, the lightning
bolts, the salt to take with life
though it was always like this somewhere

the border guards endlessly increase,
like those hard-bodied ants she watches,
hatching, moving, leaving their radioactive
shells strewn on the floor

like those spiders patrolling the windowpanes,
building quadrants of belligerent silk,
more and more ruthlessly, across
the hummingbird feeder,
the gateway to the stairs,
pincering traceries between trees,
the mouth of the river

the path to the lake,
furiously
modernizing their barbed wire every breached hour

Eight hundred every month for the last year

it was July then, a decent month at any other
time, a month of heat and water, beer and
friends, beaches and parks

little pain usually

bandages of sunlight salving the eyes,
and somewhere
in someone's life it's still true

they'll look forward to the cafés till late,
and talk till sleep,
and sobering up tomorrow to begin again
the romance with streets and sidewalks, jubilant
immortal electricity

yet, this figure, eight hundred every month
for the last year, and one hundred
and twenty in a brutal four days,
things, things add up

IV

i


At Al Rifai Mosque,
the Shah of Iran lies on an onyx floor

entering the mihrab,
the guard offers to sing so we can hear
the perfect acoustic of the burial chamber,
then cups the most beautiful music
from his throat, the call to prayer,
you would think the onyx would break,
or melt away,
the Shah awake and beg forgiveness
for all the despicable years

but no,
the guard releases his face
from his hands,
and returns to the commerce of such an exchange,
his sweet voice for baksheesh,
we paid him gladly,
how much would be enough
for the ruin of his life,
singing to the Shah, hourly

we told him he was beautiful,
at least that

ii

Something else, more happened there

once among the silversmiths,
among the old work of ornamentation,
the shining pain of metal and hammer,
a voice called to me, "Welcome back, Cousin,"
familiar like the sound of water,
rain on a roof or the sea outside a door,
"Welcome, Cousin, it's been a long time,
we have a lot to talk about,
you could be a spy from Upper Egypt

come back alone tomorrow,
we have a lot to say to each other,"

and yes, he could have been my cousin,
and was

In that whole place with everything
for sale

he tried to sell me nothing,
only our genealogy
needing to be polished,
spun over so much suspicion and time,
the silver on the shelves was worthless between us

he smelled of some perfume,
some secret room that thunder makes
when it claps and moves across skies,
of dust that ants accumulate
going about the long business
of gnawing the world away,

and sand so fine it's air

I wanted to go back, take

his hand, eat from it, but,
that was, would be, another life,
and all our rumours would collide and
take that moment away from us when
he called me "Cousin," when cousin
came from both our mouths
and was a warning and a lie, and
a soft meeting and a love

all the time I remained in Cairo,
his papery voice
caressed my cheek,
though I never returned to his small

silver place

and then I think he might have disappeared,
never existed

or never called me "Cousin"
that word is more than father sister brother
mother, clasping what is foreign whole,
all the time nevertheless,
I left him to himself

the ringing metal of his shop, the
bracelets, anklets, rings done, he said,
in the old ways,
the speckles of argentum on his tongue and brow,
his slippers on the wooden floor, the time
you know, when something falls so perfectly
from your hands

I needed nothing from the market

after that, no scarves, no perfume bottles,
no nuts, no directions to all the gates of Cairo,
no souvenirs of ancient Egypt
other than the time we'd spent in some life,
before and since,
this charm of ours as I've said before

it meets you sometimes
on a hot mountain road or in a cool silver shop,
its startling purposes,
its imperishable beckoning grace,
so unexpected,
so merciful

iii

The day you left the air broke
into splinters,
all night before the tree outside
held its breath,
the windows ached,
the newspapers whimpered unread,
old lovers, unknowing, staggered
in doorways,
We should gather rivers for you,
the Layou, the Niger, the St. Lawrence
should weep now,
we should call storms,
our grief will dry lakes,
this city should spring hibiscus
in late winter when your name
is said, full subways and streetcars
should sprout wings and fly
urgently to your side,
You knew the world,
its weather scraping our skins,
we hear you in our sleep, wild
as verses of autumn maple

We should carry you
to that country you dreamed
for us, where your liquid voice
is astonishing
If we sing here like crickets,
as perfectly, if we fill all rooms
with silence, you would return then,
or tell us how it is where you are,
how we could dilute bitter things
and acrid cities; how
to strain sorrow through our hands,
then mount demonstrations against
your death,
will you send word
in letters, in goldenrod leaflets
in spiders' threads or how we used to
at night – with buckets of glue –
on light posts,
till then Marlene,
we will fix petals of you to our eyes


*to Marlene Green*

iv


Everywhere,
out the window the muezzin singing
reaches the upper leaves of deserted
Cairo trees,
heard too the cheery stupidity of cellphones,
it was another December, dusty, late, the Sahara sprays,
the men, all men, heads bruised
with passion, or grief or conviction
or failure at noticing absences,
such deliberateness

noticed only men,
except one night in Khan el-Khalili,
a sexual thing,
covered in the film of a garment

blind, held, and desired

the man smiling, his own small hand
strong on hers, his own small frame,
a cage,
she, of course she, small too, red,
if that colour can be more burdened in the carnal,
so, red, why waste another one,
her urgency too, to become,
wanted, the poise in being wanted,
the market, lit as it is at night,
not that creation of light bulbs and wires,
but Cairo, awake,
then their incandescence, desire and desired
defeating each other, his hand again
on the ephemera of her, she dragged and willing,
everywhere

modernity for everything but this

V

i

so you find yourself anywhere
selling toys, fake roses, in the Piazza della Scala,
to the privileged, among them
a poet
you find yourself anywhere
reading Neruda, ventriloquist, to the second
millennium, *we exhausted so much on useless destruction*

always three policemen haunt our piazzas,
*interpretazione simultanea, ola preti*

it's better, the elliptical roses,
mechanical universes,
some escaped
could share life on the surface

she needed someone like that, elliptical,
and as usual the fucking Americans came,
strafing her meditation on things,
wanting, wanting, a chair, a space,
the two of them so fragile and alone in Europe,
talking loud,
arguing about the wine

you find yourself, any one,
anyone
you say it's all bullshit, it all
doesn't matter, *U.S. engagement in*
*Afghanistan* ribbons its way along TV screens,
you wonder, was this the same telecast
so many years ago,
uranium enriching in your stomach,
delicate postules

these monuments that survive
everywhere, in essence signs of the most brutal
among us, look at the cornices,
the fretwork, evenly taken for love
or reverence, if we sum it up,
if what we have now is the result,
what else was it but something hard,
some small-mindedness

hollowing out the steeples, the domes,
scarring the minarets
look now, the hordes of us collecting
at the windows,
the sermons of politicians,
their corporate benedictions

ii

Sarkozy will say, in months to come,
they must "pressure clean" the "rabble"

everywhere they say, "We come to work
with our coffins on our backs,"
at the Indian ports where they break ships,
the poor holes in Poland digging coal
for the black market

I wish I had beautiful legs
to get me to another planet,
to run in the lustrous substances of all that's left out,
all that may have,
to wake up at 5:25 a.m. to the business of birds,
the discredited physics of Christianity and Islam

iii


the gruesome things that settle
at the bottom of the brain,
there are children whose hearing's
been ruined already by the noise
of this,
she heard one today, veiled, on her cell-
phone say, "Tell that dumb bitch to get it."

sick modernity ciphers sick tribalism
everywhere

over in St. Elizabeth the sea was boiling
over the rocks, the unreplenishing coral
waking up, driving again, this time through a dawn
turned over, burning cars,
the same three policemen, a road,
the rain two nights before, eternal

iv

She's travelled such hours,
sat in the merciful transience of trains
hurrying,
each hotel room she checks
the news, and again that useful colour
of fire leapt to her bed from cars incinerated
in a market this morning,
from these rooms she sorts out the bodies
on Iraqi streets, this time
forty, then in Milan twenty-four
and in Florence thirty or so, with
sixty wounded, then twelve, then two,
in all one hundred or so in one week,
no television back in Venice, the damp
room distracted her from the inventory

V

The men here are plasma,
they collapse into video games, Palm Pilots,
remedies against dreams

*let us simply recognize*
*happiness as soon as it shows itself*

they declare themselves innocent of all events,
those that have happened and those to come,
everything
they examine the evidence against themselves
and suggest the victims cunning

they found themselves good,
down to the last general and secretary
of state

vi

rain fell,
the seas on the south coast rose,
one suicide bomber on Hafa Street smoked a cigarette,
one took care of an itch over his right eye,
not as a final act but a simple one,
reflexive

vii


the body keeps thinking it will return
to its vigour, it will receive phone calls,
and run to the corner with pamphlets,
a headband and a leather-stringed jacket,
to spread the news

tomorrow then she'll buy a mirror,
hang it in the room where the woodcuts
hang, the manifestations of the poet
in Chinese opera, two warriors, one musician,
one six-armed spear-bearing tumbler,
pendant,
in paper, the inability to fall or for that matter
hang on to bone, to crushed ear, to banked light, to ease

viii


She's afraid of killing someone today,
picked up the laundry, ate pasta,
and a citrus tart,
bought a book, drove a street,
all the while, sun in her left eye,
its usual butter of fall lindens,
maple bleeding, her hand
on the wheel,
looking back, in case it was someone
she'd killed, someone she'd hit,
infected with the afternoon

ix

your sources are compromised. didn't you
read my note. A spare room, a talkative
and secretive friend, a map out of
hell . . . not inured either, only one day a week . . .
the news is always
exaggerated. Cut it in half, divide it by four,
and subtract it from itself.
Information all has to do with location,
you know that. so tired of reading
for good signs. the chatter, chatter, chatter,
the applause for nothing. I sleep
with Sun Tzu
under my pillow. But if you don't have a room
well okay then
tell me of a pretty
place near the end of May
much love

x

Consider then the obliteration of four restaurants,
the disappearance of sixty taxis each with one passenger
or four overcrowded classrooms, one tier of a football
stadium, the sudden lack of, say, cosmeticians

or mechanics, a pedestrian intersection at lunchtime,
ostentatiously
vanished, two or three hospital waiting
rooms, the nocturnal garbage collectors gone

tearful kindergartens perhaps two or so, a city
of window washers, the mournful feast of Catholics
who march for Senhor Santo Cristo dos Milagros

tenacious too the absence and impossibility of names

let us all deny our useless names in solidarity
with these dead dinner guests and pedestrians,
and anonymously dead mechanics, and desultory
children and passengers, and those faceless cosmeticians

xi


she's never liked twilight, you know,
when it comes, it only confirms
we've failed at everything
again,
it only arrives to insist,
what a waste,
it says, I at least end things, I
understand perfection, deep
at its source it isn't power,
nothing so small, so edible
there, it is immaculate possibility

VI

It's August now, the light is deeper,
the sky explosive with rains,
a turning, turning the body of the world
toward a darkness, a sleep, no,
sleep would be forgiving

last night, late August,
Katrina's wet wing flapped, dishevelled
against the windows like great damp feathers,
she brushed the alleyways, the storm shutters,
I felt the city she had carried away,
drowned and stranded New Orleans,
anyway, she was finished,
a ruffed foot, a quilled skirt trailing off

like what billions of rainless universes do we kill
just stepping through air, what failing cultures
submerge under a breath

word on the street is that God sent Katrina
as a lesson in destruction,
lucky I'm not any kind of believer,
a taxi driver told me this, then the hairdresser,
then the old Italian ladies who peddle Jesus

when I tell them I'm an atheist they see
an opportunity for conversion

they want some single story, the story of my life,
I say this big world is the story, I don't have any other,
they offer me the immured peace
of Christianity,
and an address in Pennsylvania to send money,
they always win, these soothing ladies,
I haven't the courage to tell them we're fucked,
and they, unfortunately, will have a reason for that

though the birds of the world know this,
the banded pitta, the mangrove pitta, the bulbul,
the iora, the red-naped and scarlet-rumped

trogon, the fire-tufted barbet, flame back, philentoma,
the rufous-throated wren babbler, I tell them,

they, the birds feel this, the wingbeat,
the feathered work of greed,
this shorn planet,
the hoary-throated barwing, the greater adjutant,
the crake, the alliterative blue-bearded bee-eater,
it's clear to them,
they all must set a fire to the earth,
you see, they're saying, what would it be without birds,
what if we spread extinction, transform blood
to other tender fluids

listen to all the laughing thrushes,
striated, white throated, orange headed, all
the plain backed, blackened, chestnut, cocoa,
summoning oblivions, raining disasters

after all, how many vows of death or endless death
for endless peace have I heard from the wingless,
the flightless? The gulls, the owls, the grouses

the stalks, the larks, the finches have had it too,
with sightlessness, such clarity,
the scientists
are intent on dreamy financial answers,
but I know the suicidal skill of insurrection,
self-slaughter hunched in veins, the skull's
fever, the tissues' elations,
I too am waiting for the flutter of another century,
treading water near that meagre strip of land,
stooping there, the noise even closer

VII

On reading this someone will say
God, is there no happiness then,
of course, tennis matches and soccer games,
and river song and bird song and
wine naturally and some Sundays

and some highways with the relief of water
and wild flowers at the end,
and fresh snapper and wild salmon,
though that all depends on killing something,
and the eagerness of children and their certainty,
look how they try to walk straight

the surface of the earth, how it keeps springing back,
for now, and the irregular weather of hurricanes,
tsunamis, floods, sunlight on any given day,
anywhere, however disastrous at least magnificent

and moments when you rise to what you might be,
bread,
the girls and boys you saw in Cairo,
their hands and mouths
full, and the way a woman stands
when you meet her at an unexpected corner,

anywhere, the one that blue morning in Les Coteaux,
the one on the way
to Firenze with the baby on the train,
and the flight and dive of pelicans, the scent
of sandalwood and the scent of mangoes
when they grow black,
great ravens lifting north

and sand again, the day you realize it's stone
worn down, how long that must take,
yes, of course, there's sitting still,
and reading or merely cleaning the steps
to the little veranda,
observing the certain movement of great ants

the longitude of hours, their roiling ascent and fall,
or the latitude of palms, what makes them
appear at certain temperatures, and

men, at 5 a.m. with lunch boxes waiting,
in cool mornings at intervals of domestic road,
to go do some mindless work, how they crouch
in their clothes,
willing the truck to arrive or meet
with catastrophe, let this be the morning of the end
of the world, they pray,
there's something of a beauty there

at how one flees at the appearance of mosquitoes,
all right, the nightclubs, the bars, the dancehalls,
we all know, keeping in mind
the drunk recrimination on a life wasted,
that's common, no matter where you are,
and people who somehow make a music

come out of nothing,

yellow, there's a thing,
and something edible in a desert, or perhaps
the inedibility of deserts,
an engine on a vacant road, someone who says,
don't worry, when you need it, rain,
rain is the happiest of weathers

bicycles, great inventions even if you never
learned to ride, and coffee,
plain and hot, again at 5 a.m.
a boat, even a wrecked and wretched boat
still has all the possibilities of moving

a stick, when you're walking through
an unknown forest, so defensive, so stable,
yet blithe like a feral dog

the dancehalls, were
the dancehalls mentioned before, their capacities
for joy, the way you can't be false there

it shows, because dancehalls want nothing,
do what you like, pretend if you want, it
doesn't matter, no one to lie to there,
you can either dance or you can't

feet, their innovativeness, look how
many things they do and how open-minded

sleep, sleep is infinitely this, and waking
up, involuntary both, outside one's help,
circadian and residential, the body must,
weighed down
only by the revolutions
of the earth's incandescence and gloaming

safety pins, time and time again, time and time again
dirt, very solid whatever it is, then periwinkle,
it flourishes regardless, mimosa, most of all,
needled, flowering, vigilant, every resistant thing
in one

so yes, there's that and parcels addressed
to you from foreign countries, their smell,
of dresses and books and someone's thoughts

speaking of drunk recrimination, nothing
wrong with that,
at least it's an examination
of things past,
pity it's only fools that do it,
caught, unlike the powerful, in the immediate
effects of their ego or anger or greed

where do they spit up, those others, whatever
bile they have, so dangerous it burns the world
to dust, it devastates hospitals and scant dreams,
ask them
about happiness, not me, why should
I know how to dance and sing in the middle of it all,
okay, okay this list is not so exhausted yet

guitars then, like Hendrix and Santana,
Kongar-ool Ondar and Tanya Tagaq Gillis, throat
singing
Jali Nyama Suso playing kora, Mariza again,
singing fado,
Fela, immortal, the whole of music, the whole of it

the off-key voices in church basements and showers,
the always misinterpreted sounds of popular songs,
five Indian boys in a car listening to bangara,
the traffic jam
where we met this summer,
in the middle of all that killing

the scratching of a needle on a record,
a sample of James Brown and the Fatback Band,
squirrels in the eaves of a house going about
their business,
ground doves fluttering from tree to lemon tree

all this, black butterflies and flying ants,
rain ants, the many times that rain is mentioned here,
candle flies, poui falling

this composition that nature makes, the theories
of hummingbirds and beavers,
agoutis
and armadillos, morrocoys and one-inch pandas,
all different, don't be mistaken, they're not simple

not simple as the ways to kill them, far more
complicated,
but let's leave nature for a while
how can we, yes, let's not essentialize the only
essential thing, it doesn't work, it fails often,
fails, fails whom

and so, barrios and slums, crazy, crazy places,
violent too sometimes but there happiness
is a light post, a scar, stigmata, blazing
in every hand and water, a passport

being screams there, the jangling of intense limbs,
the expiration of any breath, its succeeding intake,
the surprised and grateful lungs

you have to measure this also there, the degrees
of the eyelashes, the width of the thumb and forefinger,
going over old newspapers, old clothes, old cans,
the wreckage of other people's lives
which is your boon,
when a day ends again the body's exhaustion,
if it comes, that's success

grackles, to return, and the yellow-crested
oropendola's chromatic notes, a flock of
dragonflies so blue you think, a dizzy spell

exquisite and contiguous, never alighting
in one place too long, the unsteadiness
of strangers, driftwood, one coastline

Marigot,
very long ago, unbathable, impassable,
smudged ochre, redundant to say rock, and yes

coastlines in general, especially from the ferry
between Vancouver and Galliano, one woman
Marlene, living, her hand pulling the strands of hair
at her temple, unravelling all the political
questions

four devotees mourning Nina Simone,
drinking wine and listening to "See-line
Woman," recalling where they were in their life
when she sang this, which city, which club, when
they first saw her as if they'd seen themselves

some lovers of course, the way they made you
laugh, the way they held their heads,
then too the relief of their leaving, of course

slowness, weeding gardens if you
have them, if not a small vinous plant, portable,
to place on a trellis when you get one, both naturally
if working in a field is not your regular job

in that case it's backbreaking, arthritic, a foul aura
surrounds you
then, standing, that move perfected by another species
one million years ago, is perfect, and gardens an eyesore

some words can make you weep,
when they're uttered, the light rap of their
destinations, their thud as if on peace, as if on cloth,
on air, they break all places intended and known

soft travellers

happiness is not the point really, it's a marvel,
an accusation in our time,
and so is this, Monday, February 28th, one
hundred and fourteen, Tuesday, August 16th, ninety
Wednesday September 14th, one hundred and eighty-
two, Friday November 18th, eighty
these were only the bloodiest days in one year,
in one place

there are atomic openings in my chest
to hold the wounded,

besides the earth's own
coiled velocities, its meteoric elegance,
and the year still not ended,
I have nothing soothing to tell you,
that's not my job,
my job is to revise and revise this bristling list,
hourly

## ACKNOWLEDGEMENTS

The lyric fragments on page 8 are from the following songs: "The Times They Are A-Changin'" by Bob Dylan; "Say It Loud, I'm Black and I'm Proud" by James Brown; "Revolution" by The Beatles; "We Shall Overcome" by Zilphia Horton, Frank Hamilton, Guy Carawan, and Pete Seeger; "Mercedes Benz" by Janis Joplin; and "Inner City Blues (Make Me Wanna Holler)" by Marvin Gaye.

The lyric fragments on page 10 are from "Te recuerdo Amanda" by Víctor Jara.

The list of reported civilian deaths on page 23 is from the Iraq Body Count project.

The lines from Pablo Neruda's "The Masks" on page 67 and "Spikes of Wheat" on page 73 are taken from *2000* by Pablo Neruda, translation by Richard Schaaf. Copyright © 1997 by Pablo Neruda and Fundación Pablo Neruda. Translation copyright © 1997 by Richard Schaaf. Used by permission of Azul Editions.